Animal Math
Comparing with Cats

Tracey Steffora

Heinemann
LIBRARY

Chicago, Illinois

© 2014 Heinemann Library
an imprint of Capstone Global Library, LLC
Chicago, Illinois

To contact Capstone Global Library please
phone 800-747-4992, or visit our web site,
www.capstonepub.com

Edited by Daniel Nunn, Abby Colich, and Sian
Smith
Designed by Joanna Hinton-Malivoire
Picture research by Elizabeth Alexander
Production by Victoria Fitzgerald
Originated by Capstone Global Library Ltd
Printed and bound in China by Leo Paper
Products Ltd

17 16 15 14 13
10 9 8 7 6 5 4 3 2 1

**Library of Congress Cataloging-in-
Publication Data**
Steffora, Tracey.
Comparing with cats / Tracey Steffora.
        pages cm.—(Animal Math)
Includes bibliographical references and index.
ISBN 978-1-4329-7559-3 (hb)
ISBN 978-1-4329-7566-1 (pb)
1. Correlation (Statistics)—Juvenile literature. 2.
Cats—Juvenile literature. 3. Felidae—
Juvenile literature. 4. Variation (Biology)—
Juvenile literature. I. Title.
  QA276.13.S74 2014
  519.5'37—dc23   2012049398

Acknowledgments
The author and publisher are grateful to the
following for permission to reproduce
copyright material: Shutterstock pp.4, 5, 7, 8, 9,
14, 17, 20 (© Eric Isselee), 4 (© Kirill Vorobyev),
6, 9 (© Iakov Filimonov), 9, 10, 11, 13 (© Katrina
Elena), 11, 12, 13 (© Robert Eastman), 12, 13 (©
Ultrashock), 15, 17 (© Albie Venter), 16, 17 (©
Tatiana Morozova), 18, 19 (© Sari Oneal), 18, 19
(© Stu Porter), 20 (© Viorel Sima), 21 (© Steve
Wilson), 21 (© Andreas Gradin); Superstock
pp.19 (Gerard Lacz / age fotostock).

Front cover photograph of a kitten reproduced
with permission of Shutterstock (© Lana
Langlois).
Front cover photograph of a lion and front
and back cover photographs of a caracal
reproduced with permission of Shutterstock (©
Eric Isselée).

We would like to thank Elaine Bennett for her
invaluable help in the preparation of this book.

Every effort has been made to contact
copyright holders of any material reproduced
in this book. Any omissions will be rectified in
subsequent printings if notice is given to the
publisher.

Contents

Some words are shown in bold, **like this**. You can find them in a glossary on page 23.

Comparing Cats

There are many types of cats. Some cats are wild. Some cats are pets. Cats live all over the world. There are many ways cats are alike and different.

We **compare** things to see how they are the same and how they are different. Let's compare some cats!

Comparing Size

Look at the **size** of this tiger! Size is how big or small something is. The tiger is the largest of all the cats.

This caracal is also large, but it is smaller than the tiger.

This little kitten is the smallest of all!

largest

smaller

smallest

Now **compare** the **size** of all three.

Comparing Weight

We **weigh** things to find out how heavy they are. Look at this house cat. Its weight is about 10 pounds.

One pound is about the same weight as a football.

bobcat

This bobcat weighs about 30 pounds.
It is heavier than the house cat.

The cougar **weighs** about 110 pounds.
It is heavier than the bobcat.

cougar

In fact, it is heavier than the bobcat
and the house cat put together!

Look at the graph

The Weight of Different Animals

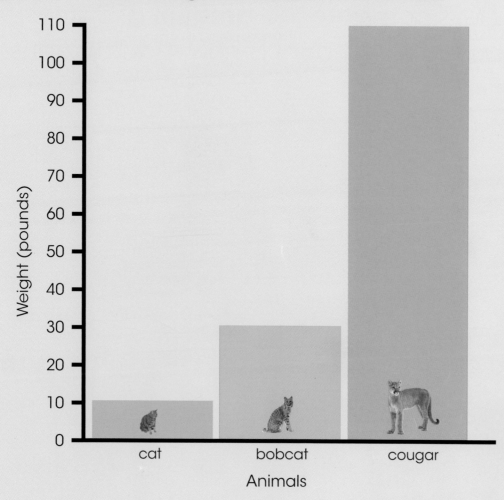

Compare the cats. The house cat is the lightest. The cougar is the heaviest.

Comparing Amounts

Now let's **compare** the **amount** of babies in each **litter**. Amount is how many there are of something.

1

2

3

4

5

This lynx has a litter of five **cubs**.

This cheetah has a litter of two cubs.

This lioness has a **litter** of three **cubs**.

Look at the graph

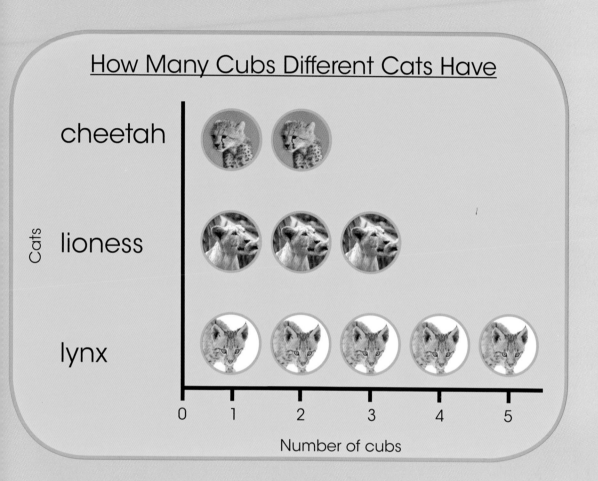

How Many Cubs Different Cats Have

Cats

cheetah

lioness

lynx

0   1   2   3   4   5

Number of cubs

The lynx has the most cubs.
The cheetah has the fewest cubs.

Comparing Speed

Look at this house cat run. It is fast! Its top **speed** is about 30 miles per hour. Speed is how fast or slow something is.

mph stands for miles per hour

This cheetah is much faster! Its top speed is about 70 miles per hour. That is as fast as a car on a highway!

Look at the graph

The Top Speed of Different Animals

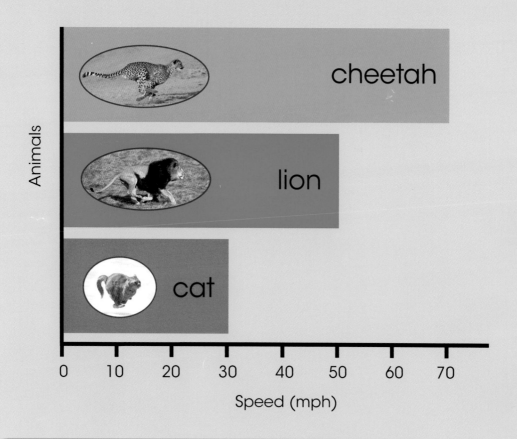

Is the lion faster or slower than the cheetah?

Answer on page 22.

You Compare

Which cat is heavier? Which cat is lighter?

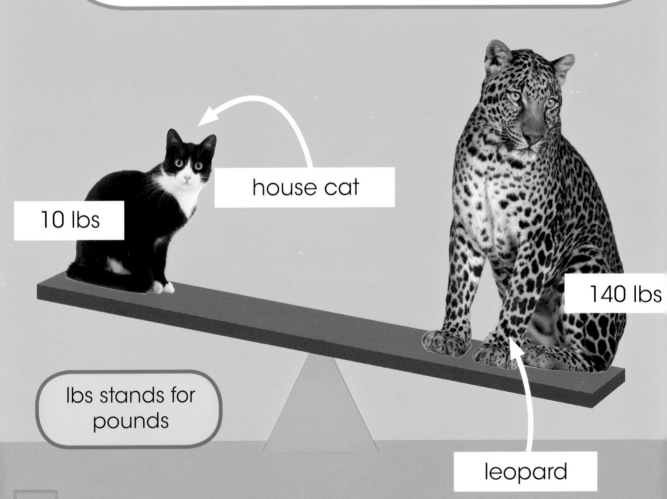

house cat

10 lbs

140 lbs

lbs stands for pounds

leopard

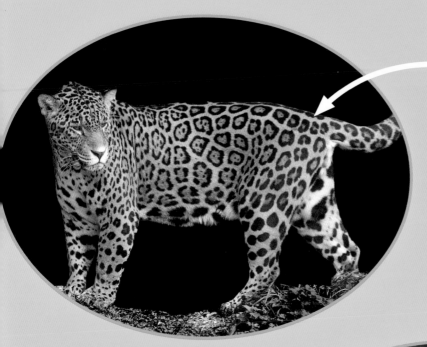

jaguar

fishing cat

Which cat is larger?

Which cat is smaller?

Answers on page 22.

21

Cat Facts

- A group of cats is called a clowder.

- All kittens and **cubs** have blue eyes when they are born.

- Cats use their tails to balance and to communicate with each other.

- A cougar is also called a puma, Florida panther, mountain lion, or catamount.

- Only four cats can roar—lions, tigers, leopards, and jaguars!

page 21: The jaguar is larger. The fishing cat is smaller.

page 20: The leopard is heavier. The house cat is lighter.

page 19: The lion is slower than the cheetah. In fact, the cheetah is the fastest animal on land!

Answers

Math Glossary

amount how many there are of something

compare look at two or more things to see how they are the same and how they are different

size how big or small something is

speed how fast or slow something is

weigh to measure how heavy something is

Cat Glossary

cub the baby of a big cat, for example a young lion or a young tiger

litter a group of baby animals that are born at the same time

Teaching Notes

Measurement is a very visible and practical part of children's lives, and it intrinsically involves comparison. This title supports children's ability to compare attributes in order to measure size, weight, amount, and speed. The use of charts and graphs further supports the ability to organize, interpret, and display measurement data.

Use this title to further support core measurement and data standards:

- Discuss different tools, such as rulers and balance scales, and how they are used when measuring. Have children choose two objects from their desk (such as an eraser and a pencil), and discuss what attributes they might use to compare these objects (length, weight, etc.). Encourage them to use tools to make these measurements and record the results. Then, have them continue this activity with other objects in the classroom.

- Build on the measurement activity above by having children write sentences using comparative language (e.g., "The pencil is longer than the eraser." or "The eraser is heavier than the pencil.")

- Examine how the pictograph on page 17 is used to compare amount. Make a class pictograph of birthdays by displaying a chart with the months of the year labeled. Ask children to draw a picture of themselves on a sticky note. Then, have children place the sticky note in the column indicating the month of their birthday. Interpret the data with the class, comparing which month has the most birthdays, the fewest, etc.

Related Common Core Standards

CCSS.Math.Content.K.MD.A.1   CCSS.Math.Content.1.MD.A.1

CCSS.Math.Content.K.MD.A.2   CCSS.Math.Content.1.MD.A.2

CCSS.Math.Content.K.MD.B.3   CCSS.Math.Content.1.MD.C.4

CCSS.Math.Content.K.CC.C.6